My First Book about the Alphabet of Birds
Extra Large Edition

Amazing Animal Books
Children's Picture Books

By Molly Davidson

Mendon Cottage Books

JD-Biz Publishing

Read More Amazing Animal Books

Purchase at Amazon.com

Download Free Books!
http://MendonCottageBooks.com

Introduction

There are over 3 billion different kinds of birds in the World, which fit into over 10,000 different species categories.

 **is for an Albatross.**

They have the largest wingspan of any living bird, which can span up to 11 feet 4 inches.

They can coast for several hundred miles without flapping their wings even once!

 is for a Bird of Paradise.

markaharper1 © <u>Wikimedia Commons</u>

There are over 36 different species in the category of Birds of Paradise, all with brightly colored feathers, and who all live in New Guinea and the surrounding islands.

B is also for a Bee-Eater Bird.

Bee-Eaters eat mostly honey bees and wasps; this is where they get their name from.

They live in large groups, called colonies, in burrows usually on the side of cliffs.

 **is for a Crane.**

Some cranes will travel over 500 miles in one day, in search of food.

They build their nests in marshy swamps, where they lay two eggs that hatch in about 30 days.

C is also for a Cockatoo.

Cockatoos are a popular pet, but if they get bored they start to destroy whatever is in their cage.

 **is for a Dove.**

Doves are a symbol of love, peace, and harmony.

They can live almost anywhere in the World, except extra dry deserts and the freezing Polar Regions.

E is for an Eagle.

Eagle's have such good eyes they can see a rabbit from over 2 miles away.

Golden eagles in Greece will catch turtles and drop them from high in the air, which breaks their shell, so they can eat their insides.

E is also for an Emu.

An emu has two eyelids, one for blinking and the other which keeps dust and sand out.

They have very strong legs which they use for running and kicking their predators.

 **is for a Falcon.**

Peregrine Falcons are the fastest animals on the planet, when they dive down they can get to speeds of 180 mph (290 km/h).

F is also for a Flamingo.

Flamingos eat shrimp which is the reason their feathers turn different colors of pink.

They can stand as tall as 4 1/2 feet, but they only weigh less than 9 pounds!

When they want to rest they stand on one leg.

 is for Geese.

Geese fly 40 mph while they are migrating, but if they are in danger they can fly up to 60 mph.

The boys and the girls make different honking noises when talking to each other.

G is also for Galliformes.

Galliformes is a species of birds that includes turkeys, chickens, grouse, pheasants, and more.

H is for a Hummingbird.

Some species of hummingbirds flap their wings 90 times per second!

Their feet are so small they cannot walk on the ground and don't like to sit on a branch for very long.

I is for an Ibis.

Ibis stand about 3 1/2 feet tall.

Their noise holes are at the top of their beak, so when they are eating underwater they can still breathe.

 **is for a Jacana.**

Jacanas are also called lily trotters because they walk on the top of water over lily pads.

They have toes that are super long, up to 7 cm, which helps spread out their weight evenly helping them stay on the top of the water.

J is also for a Jay.

Jays talk by using loud screams and calls; they can copy cat, hawk, and human noises.

The father will gather food to bring back to the nest to feed his baby and their mother.

K  is for a Kingfisher.

Kingfishers can lay up to 10 eggs at a time, which both the mother and father sit on until they hatch in 3 to 4 weeks.

They mostly live in wetlands, where they eat frogs, insects, and crayfish.

K 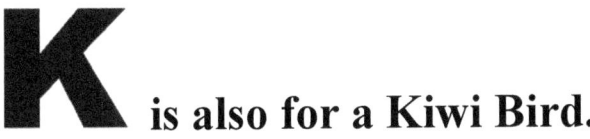 is also for a Kiwi Bird.

Kiwi cannot fly and they weigh about 2 pounds.

They are active at night, which is called being nocturnal; and to help them find food they have a great sense of smell.

L is for a Loon.

Loons spend most of their time in the water and can stay under the water for up to 5 minutes.

They have to run 100 - 600 feet before they have enough speed to fly, but once they get in the air they can fly up to 75 mph.

L is also for a Laridae, the scientific name for a Gull.

Gulls will stomp their feet on the soil, making it sound like rain, which tricks the earth worms into coming to the surface.

 **is for a Magnificent Fregatidae.**

Maros M r a z © <u>Wikiemedia Commons</u>

Magnificent fregatidae boys have a red pouch under their beak that they inflate during mating season to attract girls.

They are a seabird that lives mostly in tropical regions.

M is also for a Mallard.

Mallard boys have bright green head feathers, but the girls do not.

Once all the eggs have hatched, the mother will lead her ducklings into the water and they will never go back to the nest.

N is for a Numididae, the scientific name for a Guinea Fowl.

Guinea fowl are active in the early morning and late afternoon, they rest during the hot part of the day.

They live mostly in sub-Saharan Africa.

 **is for an Owl.**

Owls do not have teeth, so they use their sharp beak to tear their prey apart before swallowing.

Barn owls can eat up to 1,000 mice per year!

Owls have special, soft, wing feathers which help it to fly without making any noise.

O

is also for an Oriole.

Orioles stick their long beaks into fruit then open them which creates a cup, making it easy to drink the fruit's juice.

A group of orioles is called a pitch or a split.

P is for a Pelican.

Pelicans have the largest bill (beak) of any bird, which can be as long as 18 inches.

They have a throat pouch which can hold up to 3 gallons of water.

They can eat up to 4 pounds of fish per day.

P is also for a Parrot.

Parrots have 4 toes, two face forward and two face backward, which helps them hold tightly on to tree branches.

They are the only bird which can pick up food with their feet and put it in their mouth.

 **is for a Quail.**

Quails bathe in the dirt, which helps keep bugs off and their feathers clean.

They lay around 6 bright eggs which take 23 days to hatch.

They can only fly for short distances.

R is for a Roadrunner.

Roadrunners run about 20 mph and they can fly, but only for a short distance.

They will lay in the sun to get warm before they go hunting for food.

R is also for a Robin.

Robin's favorite food is earthworms.

In the cold wind, they puff up their feathers
which helps keep them warm and insulated.

Most robin's die protecting their territory.

S is for a Spheniscidae, the scientific name for a Penguin.

Penguins are unable to fly in the air, but they use their wings as flippers and are amazing swimmers.

They live where the wind chill can be as low as -76°F!

S is also for a Swallow.

Swallows fly in a zig zag pattern above the top of the water or the ground.

They build mud nests on the banks of rivers in caves and on cliffs.

Their favorite food is flies.

T is for a Toucan.

Toucans have a large brightly colored beak which has lots of tiny air pockets, these help to make it weigh less.

They spend most of their time high in the trees, where they jump from branch to branch.

T is also for a Tern.

Terns nest mostly on sandy beaches along ocean coasts.

Baby terns can fly at about 20 days old.

They live in groups, called colonies, of up to 500 birds.

U
is for an Upland Sandpiper.

Sandpipers usually hunt in small groups, but it nests with up to 100 birds.

The mother and the father both take care of the babies until they are about one month old and can fly by themselves.

 **is for a Vulture.**

Vultures fly about 150 miles per day in search of dead animal carcasses, which they eat.

Babies learn to fly when they are 6 months old.

They can live up to 60 years in the wild.

V is also for a Vaux's Swift.

Richard Crossley © <u>Wikimedia Commons</u>

Vaux' s Swift birds have bristles above their eyes which they can move to protect their eyes from the sunlight, like sunglasses.

 **is for a Woodpecker.**

Woodpeckers have a long tongue which they use to get bugs out of trees to eat.

X is for Xanthocephalus

Xanthocephalus, the scientific name for a Yellow-Headed Blackbird.

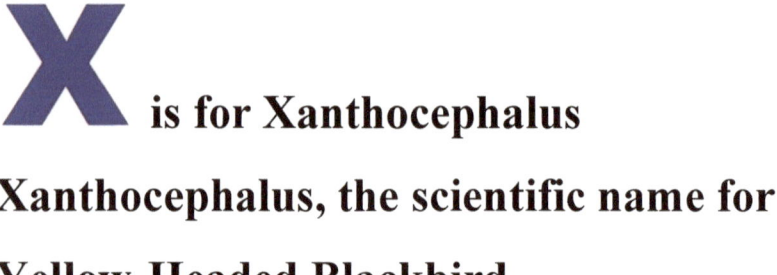

Dave Menke © <u>Wikimedia Commons</u>

Yellow-headed blackbirds live in large colonies, mostly to the west of the Great Lakes.

 is for a Yellow Canary.

Canary birds get their name from the Canary Islands off the northern coast of Africa, where they are from.

They eat seeds, berries, and insects.

Yellow canaries are a popular pet which lives for 5 - 9 years.

Z is for a Zone-Tailed Hawk.

HarmonyonPlanetEarth © <u>Wikimedia Commons</u>

Zone-tailed hawks can see 8 times better than humans.

They hunt mostly for frogs, small birds, squirrels, rabbits, snakes, and rats.

Conclusion

I hope you have enjoyed reading about many amazing birds.

One more fact, most birds have hollow wings, this makes them lighter, which makes it easier for them to fly.

Our books are available at

1. Amazon.com

2. Barnes and Noble

3. Itunes

4. Kobo

5. Smashwords

6. Google Play Books

Download Free Books!
http://MendonCottageBooks.com

Publisher

JD-Biz Corp

P O Box 374

Mendon, Utah 84325

http://www.jd-biz.com/